Original title: Moonlit Verses

Author: Kene Elistrand
Editor: Jessica Elisabeth Luik
ISBN 978-9916-39-942-2

Moonlit Verses

Kene Elistrand

Ballad of the Swaying Tides

Upon the shore where whispers dwell,
In the rhythm of the swaying tide,
Secrets in the moonlight fell,
As waves and dreams collide.

Beneath the vast, embracing sky,
Where salty tears and oceans meet,
The seagulls' lonely, plaintive cry,
Echoes in the deep's discreet.

With each ebb, with each flow,
The sand carves tales of eons past,
In timeless dance, in gentle throw,
Memories too vast to last.

The night's embrace draws shadows long,
As stars reflect on waters wide,
The ocean's heart beats strong,
Within the Ballad of the Swaying Tide.

Ascension into the Nocturnal Bloom

When day resigns, and shadows bloom,
Beneath the cloak of impending gloom,
Stars awaken in the velvet sky,
Guiding spirits as they fly.

The moon ascends, a silvery sphere,
In the nocturne, souls draw near,
Mysteries unfurled in the silken gloom,
Whispers of life in nocturnal bloom.

Through the veil of the darkest night,
Flickers of hope, in starlight bright,
Dreams ascend on the wings of owls,
In the silence that the darkness prowls.

Winds carry tales of ancient times,
In hushed tones, in whispered rhymes,
Ascending into the night's embrace,
Finding peace in the moon's grace.

Oscillating Heartbeats Synced with the Cosmic Pulse

In the vastness of the cosmic sea,
Where stars dance and galaxies breathe,
Two hearts beat in synced harmony,
With the universe's unseen sheathe.

Through the black, through the void,
In the silence, love's voice deployed,
Oscillating in a rhythm so vast,
Pulses syncing in the celestial cast.

In the fabric of space, time intertwines,
Two souls merge, where infinity dines,
Each heartbeat, a cosmic note played,
In the symphony of light and shade.

With every beat, a star is born,
In the cosmic web, love is sworn,
Vibrating in endless, boundless space,
Two hearts synced in the cosmic embrace.

Midnight's Luminous Embrace

In the realm where night skies lace,
With stars that twinkle, then embrace.
Moonlight bathes the earth below,
In a tender, silvery glow.

Velvet darkness wraps around,
Silence speaks without a sound.
The world below in slumber lies,
Underneath the watchful skies.

Gentle whispers in the air,
Midnight dreams without a care.
Luminescent love so bright,
Holding darkness with its light.

Every shadow gently sways,
In the moon's embracing rays.
Till the dawn begins to rise,
In the east, a new surprise.

Veiled in Shadows

Veiled in shadows, hidden deep,
The secrets that the night does keep.
Whispering winds in the dark,
Carry tales of an arcane mark.

Beneath the cloak of evening's guise,
Mysteries dance before our eyes.
Ephemeral, they twist and weave,
Fabric of night they conceive.

Echoes of footsteps softly tread,
Past whispers of the silent dead.
Through corridors of time untold,
In shadows, stories unfold.

Hidden worlds, obscured from sight,
Bloom beneath the cloak of night.
Veiled in darkness, they await,
The curious to investigate.

Echoes of Lunar Light

Echoes of a lunar light,
Shimmering softly through the night.
Each ray a whisper from the past,
In silver tones, shadows cast.

Ripples on a midnight pond,
To the moon and stars respond.
A dance of light on darkened hue,
A secret pathway to the blue.

Through leaves, the lunar whispers breeze,
Stories told between the trees.
A timeless serenade of peace,
Where all the earthly troubles cease.

Glimpses of the night's ballet,
In every beam that dares to stray.
Painting dreams in silvered light,
Echoes of the moon so bright.

Sapphire Hues and Silver Tides

Beneath a blanket of twilight skies,
Where sapphire hues and silver tides arise.
The moon, a beacon in the dark,
Illuminates the ocean's spark.

Waves whisper secrets to the shore,
In a rhythm, they adore.
Each ebb and flow, a tender sigh,
Underneath the starlit sky.

Marine life dances in delight,
Beneath the surface, out of sight.
Glowing softly, deep and wide,
In realms where mysteries reside.

The night's embrace, cool and wide,
Harbors dreams that deep inside,
Resonate with the ocean's song,
In sapphire hues where hearts belong.

A Glimpse Through the Shadows

Beneath the veil of the twilight beam,
A realm unseen, where shadows gleam.
Within the whisper of the trees,
Lies a secret, carried by the breeze.

Amidst the silence of the night,
Shadows dance in the pale moonlight.
A fleeting glimpse of what might be,
In the darkness, what can you see?

Through the shadows, a path unwinds,
To a place where light and dark finds.
A harmony, a silent pact,
Where mysteries become fact.

Under the watch of the silver moon,
Where dreams are whispered, and wishes bloom.
The shadows hold tales untold,
In their embrace, mysteries unfold.

Guardians of the Night

In the velvet cloak of the night they stand,
Guardians silent, across the land.
Their eyes aglow with a starry light,
Protectors they are, of the nocturnal sight.

With whispers that rustle the leaves of trees,
And the howl that rides the midnight breeze.
They move unseen, without a trace,
Keeping watch over the silent space.

Their presence felt in the gentle night,
In the calmness, in the soft moonlight.
They roam the earth, without a sound,
In their eternal duty, they are bound.

When the world is wrapped in the tranquil night,
They ensure the morning comes bright.
Guardians of the dark, so bold,
Their stories in whispers, silently told.

The Wandering Light

Across the vast, inky expanse it roams,
A wandering light, through the heavenly domes.
Across galaxies vast and wide,
In its solitude, it takes its stride.

Through constellations, it weaves its path,
A silent traveler, in the aftermath.
Past planets and stars, it makes its way,
A lone beacon, in the endless sway.

Its journey is long, through the cosmic sea,
A light that wanders, forever free.
Through the darkness, it brings a spark,
A hope, a guide, in the infinite dark.

This wandering light, so far and lone,
Its origins lost, its destiny unknown.
Yet in its glow, so faint and slight,
Lies the beauty of the endless night.

Tears of the Night Sky

Upon the canvas of the night so deep,
Where the world in silence does sleep.
The stars, they shine, and softly cry,
Tears of light, from the sky.

Each one a story, a memory old,
A tale of warmth, in the cold.
They flicker and they gently weep,
Secrets of the universe, they keep.

These tears that fall, from realms high,
Illuminating the vast, endless sky.
A silent sorrow, they seem to convey,
Of beauty lost, in the light of day.

Yet in their sorrow, there's hope so bright,
A reminder, in the darkest night.
For even the night sky cries its tears,
In the silence, where nobody hears.

Beckoned by the Hush of Night

In the velvet cloak of the endless sky,
Where whispers of the stars bid me nigh.
The moon, a beacon in realms so vast,
Guides my heart to memories, long past.

Upon the breath of the cool night air,
My thoughts untangle from daily despair.
The nocturnal peace, a soothing balm,
In the kingdom of night, I find my calm.

The hush of darkness, my solace deep,
Where dreams flutter and secrets keep.
The silent moments between each day,
A sanctuary where my hope may lay.

The night's embrace, gentle and kind,
In its quietude, solace I find.
With each star's twinkle, my sorrows fade,
Under its spell, my fears are allayed.

Threads of Silver in the Loom of Night

The moon weaves threads of silver so bright,
Through the loom of night, a glorious sight.
Each beam a path across the dark expanse,
A tapestry of light, woven by chance.

Shadows play in this nocturnal dance,
Under the stars, where dreams might advance.
The night air, filled with a mystic glow,
Carries the whispers of the spirits low.

Through the ebony tapestry, so vast,
Silver threads bind the present to the past.
In the stillness, nature sings her tune,
Beneath the watchful gaze of the moon.

This woven marvel, a sight to behold,
Tells ancient stories, in the night so bold.
Through silver threads, our fates intertwine,
In the loom of night, where stars align.

Tryst with the Night's Jewel

Under the cloak of the ephemeral night,
The diamond sky reveals its might.
The moon, a jewel in the crown of dusk,
Whispers secrets in the air, so musk.

A tryst with the night, so profound,
Where every silent whisper sounds.
In the moon's glow, mysteries unveil,
Guiding the lost, on trails now pale.

The luminous orb, mighty and bold,
Casts a silver hue, a sight untold.
Its light, a beacon for hearts astray,
Illuminates paths in a gentle way.

The night's jewel, with its tranquil blaze,
In its serene light, my spirits raise.
In its presence, my worries cease,
Beneathing the moon, I find my peace.

Illumination on the Path of Shadows

In the depth of night, where shadows play,
A lone light flickers, keeping dark at bay.
The path before me, once veiled in dread,
Now clear, where the light dares to tread.

Each step, a journey through time and thought,
By the illumination, guidance sought.
The shadows dance, but do not fright,
In the stark contrast of darkness and light.

This beacon, a guide through the unknown,
A comfort in the vast night, alone.
Where fear once reigned, now courage grows,
On the path of shadows, the light bestows.

With every shadow that fades away,
The night's dark cloak reveals the day.
In the midst of darkness, light finds a way,
Illuminating paths, where hope may stay.

Cycle of the Celestial

Upon the grand celestial sphere,
Where stars dance in harmonious grace.
Cycles of time draw near and disappear,
In the infinite, boundless outer space.

Ecliptic paths that planets weave,
Following the music of the cosmos.
Under the sun, we dream and believe,
In the night, moonlight we propose.

Galaxies whirl in majestic spins,
A ballet of light across the sky.
The cycle ends, anew begins,
In the celestial sea, we sail and fly.

Seasons change at heavens' behest,
Guiding life with gentle hand.
In the cycle, we find our quest,
And by the stars, we understand.

Day to night, and back to light,
In this cycle, hope is born.
Celestial bodies, oh so bright,
From evening until morn.

In the Realm of Twilight

In the realm of twilight, under fading light,
Shadows merge, and day meets night.
The threshold time, neither dark nor bright,
A symphony performed out of sight.

Stars peek through the velvet dusk,
As night's curtain, softly falls.
In twilight's magic, we trust and must,
Listen to the nightingale's calls.

The world in balance, of day and night,
Where secrets dwell in the gloaming light.
Twilight, the bridge of dreams' flight,
Uniting realms in silent delight.

Through the twilight, we gently tread,
Between the known and the mysteries ahead.
In this liminal space, softly led,
By the twilight's thread, we are fed.

In the realm where shadows play,
Twilight reigns in subtle sway.
Guiding us to the end of day,
In realms of twilight, we find our way.

The Scribe of Night's Secrets

Under the cloak of night, a scribe writes,
In the silence, where darkness alights.
With ink as black as the void, scribing flights,
Tales of the stars, and their eternal fights.

Each word a whisper of the night's soul,
Recording dreams, desires, and fears.
On parchment, these stories he'd scroll,
Secrets of the night, through the years.

The quill moves, under the moon's gaze,
Penning verse of love's tender grace.
In the night's embrace, his thoughts ablaze,
Capturing the beauty of time and space.

With the dawn, his task at rest,
The scribe of night, completes his quest.
In his scrolls, the night confessed,
Secrets penned, forever blessed.

As daylight breaks, his work kept secret,
The scribe of night's lore, a sacred poet.
In shadowed words, truth's sonnet,
Under the stars, his verse is set.

Tapestry of the Dark Sky

In the tapestry of the dark sky,
Stars stitch patterns with light on high.
A canvas of black, where comets fly,
Telling tales that never die.

The moon weaves silver in the night,
A gleaming thread through the dark, brings light.
In its glow, dreams take flight,
On this canvas, the heart's delight.

Constellations form stories old,
Of heroes brave and villains bold.
Across the sky, their tales are told,
In stitches of celestial gold.

Nebulas dye with colors bright,
Galaxies swirl in the absence of light.
The tapestry, a breathtaking sight,
A testament to the night's might.

In the dark sky, a silent symphony plays,
A tapestry that forever stays.
Each night, a new scene portrays,
In the cosmic weave, the universe sways.

Secrets Enscribed in the Orb of Night

In the velvet cloak of the endless sky,
Whispers dance where the shadows lie.
Moon, the guardian of night's deep lore,
Holds secrets sealed by the ancient yore.

Glowing glyphs on its silver face,
Tell tales of lost, ethereal grace.
The cratered canvas, silent and bright,
A witness to eons of celestial light.

Within its grasp, mysteries reside,
Dreams and nightmares side by side.
The orb of night, in its quiet splendor,
Guides the seeker, tender and tender.

Its light, a beacon for the heart's quest,
Illuminates the path for the unrest.
In the glow of the moon's serene embrace,
We find the courage, the darkness to face.

Reverie Under the Watchful Eye

Underneath the dome of the cosmic plains,
Stars gaze down, linking invisible chains.
The night sky, a vault of infinite eyes,
Watching over Earth with silent sighs.

In the embrace of the night's cool air,
Whispers of the ancients, felt everywhere.
The universe watches in quiet reverie,
A guardian of dreams, of every memory.

Eternal spectators of our lives' unfold,
In their gaze, a story untold.
The silent judgement, neither cruel nor kind,
In their vigil, solace we find.

We lay under the watchful eyes above,
Contemplating existence, life, and love.
In the tranquil night, a connection so rare,
With the universe, in its watchful care.

Paths Lit by the Herald of Dusk

As the sun dips low, the sky alight,
The herald of dusk begins its flight.
An amber glow casts shadows long,
Singing the day's final song.

The path ahead, unclear as night,
Becomes a trail of shimmering light.
The twilight guides with gentle hand,
Across the dimming, dusky land.

Where once the day was bright and bold,
The shades of evening now take hold.
Each step upon this twilight path,
Illuminates a mystic wrath.

The journey through the fading light,
Transforms the world before our sight.
By the herald of dusk, we're led astray,
Into the arms of the coming day.

The night's embrace, close and kind,
Reveals the pathways we sought to find.
Lit by the herald, our fears unmask,
Guiding us through dusk's gentle task.

Conversations with the Invisible

Whispers float through the empty air,
Voices of the unseen, lingering there.
Conversations with the invisible, silent and profound,
In every shadow, their words are found.

Beneath the cloak of the world unseen,
Lies the speech of what might have been.
Echoes of the past, whispers of the future,
In the language of the ethereal tutor.

Talking to the spirits that dance in the mist,
Their existence, a persistent twist.
The silent dialogue between the world and ghost,
In their company, we're never truly lost.

These conversations with the invisible throng,
Tell tales of right, tales of wrong.
In their silence, wisdom we borrow,
Guidance today, and on the morrow.

Invisible voices, clear and divine,
Offering insights, a precious sign.
In their silence, a lesson is spun,
Of battles lost, and victories won.

Sewn into the Velvet Sky

Stitched with threads of silver light,
Above, the heavens stretch so wide.
Each star a whisper in the night,
A secret, in the cosmos confide.

Gleaming needles pierce the dome,
Sewing dreams into the dark tapestry.
In this vast, celestial home,
Our hopes mirror in harmony.

Bathed in moonlight, soft and shy,
Lies the world, in slumber deep.
Underneath the stitched sky,
Dreams weave into the sleep.

Silent wishes, softly cast,
On every glowing, distant star.
In the velvet sky, vast,
Our dreams, from afar, are not so far.

With every stitch, the night is drawn,
A masterpiece of light and shade.
Until the arrival of the dawn,
In the sky, our dreams are laid.

Under the Gaze of Ancient Lights

Under the gaze of ancient lights,
We stand, mere whispers in time.
Bearing witness to endless nights,
Our stories told in silent rhyme.

The cosmos, an old, watchful sage,
Observes with a patient, knowing eye.
Each lifetime, just a fleeting page,
In the grand book of the sky.

Ancestral stars in the heavens hang,
Guiding paths with their gentle light.
Their tales, of when the world began,
Illuminate our darkest night.

We seek the wisdom of the ages past,
In every gleam that pierces through.
A connection to the vast,
Under the gaze of the ancient's view.

Our questions cast into the night,
Hoping for an echo, a return.
Under the ancient lights, so bright,
We and the cosmos, together, learn.

Reflection on the Ebony Canvas

Upon the ebony canvas, wide,
The cosmos paints with strokes of light.
Each star, a tale of pride,
Reflecting on the canvas of the night.

The moon, a beacon, fiercely bright,
Casts reflections on a sea of black.
Guiding dreamers through the night,
On their endless, wandering track.

Constellations dance in silent glee,
Telling stories old as time.
On the canvas, vast and free,
Their legends climb, in the night sublime.

The universe whispers in a hush,
Secrets on the canvas, spread.
In the quiet, a sudden rush,
Of cosmic tales, in starlight, said.

Mirrored on this darkened sheet,
Is the beauty of the endless above.
In the night, our hearts beat,
To the rhythm of stellar love.

Night's Quiet Guardian Unveiled

In the cloak of night, so deeply veiled,
Lies a guardian, quiet and grand.
Over silent lands, it has sailed,
A protector of the sleeping land.

The moon, in its solemn grace,
Watches over the world below.
Its light, a soft embrace,
Guiding those who wander, to and fro.

Through thickets dark and valleys deep,
The moonlight whispers, serene.
Guarding dreams of those asleep,
In the night, it reigns supreme.

Its glow unveils the beauty hidden,
In shadows of the night's domain.
All fears and worries, now unbidden,
Under its watch, they wane.

So here's to the guardian, silent and bold,
In the night sky, it unfolds.
Its story, in silver light, told,
A watcher, quiet, and eternally old.

Under a Silver Veil

Beneath the silver veil of night so pure,
A world awakens, gentle and demure.
Moonlight dances through the whispering trees,
Casting shadows that sway with the breeze.

Within the silence, a hidden life thrives,
Nature's quiet whispers, its soul survives.
A river mirrors the spectral moon's grace,
Guiding the lost to a serene embrace.

Stars peek through the fabric of the dark sky,
Like gems that in the deepest oceans lie.
The night's cold air, filled with a secret trust,
Carries the dreams of the day turned to dust.

Creatures roam under the celestial veil,
In their world, where daylight's memories fail.
The silver glow, a silent guardian's light,
Shelters the secrets kept far from our sight.

Secrets of the Night Sky

When dusk falls and the first star dares to gleam,
The night sky unfolds like a lucid dream.
A tapestry woven from cosmic thread,
Telling stories of the living and dead.

Planets align in an eternal dance,
Whispering secrets of chance and romance.
Galaxies spinning in silent grace,
Each a delicate, infinite embrace.

Comets blaze paths with their fiery tails,
Across the heavens, a glowing trail sails.
Asteroids wander, a celestial flock,
Carving their journey through the starry rock.

The moon, a beacon in the vast, dark sea,
Illuminates the night's mystery.
Under this canvas, so vast and so wide,
Lies the universe, with secrets inside.

Whispering Craters

On the moon's surface, silent and bare,
Lie whispering craters, secrets to share.
The footprints of explorers long gone,
Echo in nights, forever drawn.

Through telescopes, curious eyes peer,
At the quiet majesty, so clear.
A landscape forged from cosmic fire,
Holds tales of humanity's desire.

Each crater, a story told in stone,
A silent witness, eternally alone.
They speak of impacts, ancient and vast,
Histories written, shadows cast.

By day, the sun casts a glaring light,
But it's in darkness, the moon whispers take flight.
In every crater, a mystery dwells,
In every silence, a story swells.

Beyond the Dusk

As daylight bleeds into shades of rust,
Beyond horizons, in the twilight trust.
Stars awaken in the deep indigo,
A silent symphony, a cosmic show.

Whispers of dreams weave through the dark,
Guiding the lost, igniting a spark.
In the embrace of night, fears are lost,
In its vastness, our worries are tossed.

Moonlight dances on paths unseen,
Silver beams through the shadows lean.
A journey beyond, where spirits soar,
In the dusk, we find ourselves and more.

Eternal night, in its beauty, we bask,
Unveiling truths behind nature's mask.
Beyond the dusk, where mysteries dwell,
In its silence, our stories it tells.

Serenade of the Starlit

Under the canvas of the night serene,
Where starlit whispers paint the scene.
Each glow, a note in the sky's grand chart,
A celestial melody that speaks to the heart.

The moon conducts with a radiant grace,
A serenade that time cannot erase.
Constellations string chords of light,
In harmony, the universe ignites.

The breeze hums along, a soft embrace,
As shooting stars trace lines in space.
In this symphony, without a word,
The unheard beauty of the cosmos stirred.

This nocturnal hymn, so pure and clear,
Calls to the soul, drawing it near.
The night sky's song, vast and wide,
In its embrace, we quietly confide.

Quietude's Illumination

In the heart of silence, light whispers soft,
In shadowed corners, darkness aloft.
The quietude speaks, in echoes and hums,
A solace, where tranquillity becomes.

Amidst the still, a gentle glow stirs,
Illuminating thoughts, quiet as furs.
In the hush, insights brightly shine,
In the quiet, clarity is divine.

The silence, a canvas, pure and blank,
Upon which mind's brush freely sank.
With each stroke, illumination spreads,
In tranquility, the soul treads.

A beacon in silence, the heart's soft light,
Guiding through shadows, making spirits bright.
In quietude's embrace, we find our might,
In its gentle illumination, our path alight.

Painter of the Silent Night

In the cloak of night, a painter unseen,
With a palette of dreams, in the serene.
Brushing strokes of moonlight, soft and light,
On the canvas of darkness, the stars ignite.

Silhouettes cast by the midnight's charm,
Crafted with care, in the night so calm.
The whisper of the wind, an artist's sigh,
As it paints the world, beneath the dark sky.

A masterpiece unfolds, in the silent hour,
Where each shadow blooms, a nocturnal flower.
The night's quiet muse, in its tender flight,
Guides the hand that paints the silent night.

With each shade of darkness, a new hope reborn,
In the silent night, where dreams are drawn.
A solace found in the night's embrace,
In the painter's stroke, we find our tranquil grace.

Dreams Cast in Silvery Hue

In the quiet of the night, under the moon's gentle gaze,
Shadows dance in dreamy mist, a silvery hue they embrace.
Dreams weave through the whispers of the dark,
Guided by the nightingale's hark.

Stars twinkle, secrets of the heart,
Each a story, a unique part.
In dreams cast in a silvery hue,
Desires unfurl, wishes come true.

Beneath the moon's soft, calming light,
Dreamers roam in the depths of night.
In the realm where fantasies flow,
There, in the silvered moonlight, dreams grow.

Visions gleam in the tranquil pace,
Like rivers of stardust in endless space.
In this nocturnal serenity,
We find our solace, our destiny.

Solace in the Spectrum of Twilight

As day gives way to the embrace of night,
Purples and pinks in the twilight ignite.
Horizon lines bleed in colors so bright,
Offering solace, easing the fright.

In the spectrum of twilight, hearts find peace,
The hustle of day finds its release.
In colors that calm, in the gentle decrease,
Souls are bathed in a soothing grease.

The fading light, a soft, tender balm,
Eases worries, brings a comforting calm.
In twilight's spectrum, the world is a psalm,
A healing space, a spiritual qualm.

As shadows lengthen and the day ends,
Twilight whispers, its spectrum sends.
A time for healing, as darkness ascends,
In twilight's embrace, the broken mends.

Nature's canvas, alive with hue,
Twilight's beauty, forever true.
In this hour, life seems anew,
Solace found in its colorful view.

Lullabies Echoing in the Lunar Cradle

In the cradle of the night, where the moon softly gleams,
Lullabies echo, weaving through dreams.
The quiet hum of the universe's streams,
Soothes the soul, in the lunar beams.

Stars flicker like candles in the vast, velvet sky,
Their light cradling earth from on high.
Lullabies carry on the wind's gentle sigh,
Whispers of peace, in the night's lullaby.

The world rests under the moon's tender watch,
In its light, the worries of the day blotch.
Lullabies flow, a comforting touch,
In the lunar cradle, nothing feels too much.

The night wraps its arms in a soft embrace,
In its tranquility, we find our place.
Lulled by the moon's loving grace,
In dreams, our spirits dance and trace.

As the night unfolds, the earth in repose,
Under the moon, everything decomposes.
Lullabies whisper, the day's close,
In the lunar cradle, peace flows.

Frost Kissed by Starlight

In the hush of the winter night, frost kissed by starlight,
The world sparkles, clad in a dress of white.
Each crystal a reflection of the night's bright,
A world bathed in a serene, glowing light.

The trees stand guard, in the cold air, so still,
The forest whispers, embracing winter's chill.
Frost kissed by starlight, the world seems to fill,
With a magic that gives the heart a thrill.

Beneath the stars, the frozen earth gleams,
In the embrace of the night, it dreams.
A landscape transformed by icy streams,
Under the starlight, it all redeems.

Starlight dances on the snow's pristine face,
In each sparkle, a story, a grace.
Frost kissed by starlight, in the quiet space,
Nature's artistry, the night's embrace.

In the silence of the winter's night,
Where frost and starlight share their light,
Peace descends, pure and bright,
In this frozen moment, everything's all right.

Glow of the Night's Mistress

In midnight's embrace, under the sable sky,
Above where dreams dare to fly and lie,
Gleams the moon, the night's mistress so bright,
The silver guardian of the tranquil night.

Her beams cast forth an ethereal glow,
Illuminating paths where darkness flow,
The whispering winds in her light do dance,
Within her realm, all find their chance.

Each phase, a chapter, a story anew,
In her glow, the world's hues imbue,
A reflection of the sun's daylit fire,
Yet in her touch, an independent desire.

In the dance of the cosmos, she sways,
A beacon through the night's quiet maze,
Guiding the lost, the wanderer's heart,
In her glow, from shadows, we depart.

The mistress of night, with a silvered lace,
In her embrace, finds the earth's solace,
Under her watch, the world softly sighs,
In the glow of the night's mistress, under the skies.

Shimmer on the Darkened Path

When the sun dips below the world's wide brim,
And the light fades to gray, and vigor grows dim,
The path ahead, a shadowed, daunting track,
With the night's cloak draped upon one's back.

Yet fear not, for there comes a gentle shimmer,
A glint of hope in the gloom does glimmer,
Footsteps light upon the ground doth tread,
Guided by the stars overhead.

Through thicket and thorn, the path winds and weaves,
Shrouded in the tales that the darkness conceives,
But onward marches the sojourner's soul,
Driven by dreams that the night does extol.

And lo! The path's end, a sight to behold,
Lit by the moon's silver, and stars bold,
No longer shall the wanderer roam,
For in the shimmer, they have found their home.

The night, once a veil of uncertainty,
Now a canvas of celestial beauty,
Each step, each breath, under the sky's vast dome,
Is illuminated, on this darkened path home.

The Solitude of Celestial Light

Beyond the clamor of our worldly plight,
Lies the solitude of celestial light,
Where stars whisper across the void so vast,
Tales of the future, present, and past.

Amidst the cosmos, a silent ballet,
Galaxies dance, in dark matter's sway,
The nebulae their nursery and grave,
A universe majestic and brave.

The solitude, a sanctum so pure,
Offers perspective, a cosmic lure,
To gaze upon infinity's face,
Is to find one's self, and one's place.

Though we are but specks within the night,
To the stars, we are beacons of light,
Reflecting back the solitude we seek,
In the celestial, a bond unique.

So when you stand under the night's expanse,
And the universe's majesty you glance,
Remember the solitude's embrace,
A celestial light, in the never-ending space.

Echoes of a Silvered Sigh

In the hush of night, under moon's quiet gaze,
Where shadows blend and the ethereal plays,
The echoes of a silvered sigh are heard,
A melody, soft, like the beat of a bird.

Each note a ripple on the still, dark lake,
Spreading far beyond where we partake,
A testament to the silence it breaks,
In its resonance, a solemnity awakes.

This sound, a beacon through the night's embrace,
Leads wayward souls to a tranquil place,
Where hearts can rest, free from despair,
In the echoes of a sigh, solace they share.

The moon, a silent witness to this rite,
Basks the world below in her gentle light,
And in her gaze, the sigh finds its flight,
A silvered breath, in the depths of night.

Thus, when darkness falls, and all seems lost,
And we count our troubles, a growing cost,
Listen for the sigh, in the moonlight's gleam,
For in its echoes, hope can redeem.

Footprints on the Dewy Meadow

In the early morn's gentle glow,
A path untrodden, soft, and low,
Beneath the sky's light, rosy spread,
Footprints weave where dewy grasses lay their head.

Beside the brook, under the willow's sweep,
The footprints dance, they run, they leap,
Over the meadow, under the sun's first beams,
In this quiet place, where nature dreams.

Through fields of green, lush and wide,
Past flowers that in the morning hide,
The footprints tell a tale so sweet,
Of solitude and joy, where earth and sky meet.

Yet, as the day wears on, and shadows grow,
The dewy trail begins to slow,
Until at last, in the evening's cool embrace,
The footprints vanish, without a trace.

Whispers Beyond the Darkness

When light fades, and shadows fall,
Beyond the darkness, I hear your call,
Whispers drift, from unseen lips,
Guiding me on a celestial trip.

Through the ebony veil that night has spun,
Our secret language, known to none,
Speaks of love, and hidden fears,
In whispers that only the heart hears.

In the deep silence, where dreams are born,
Before the canvas of the world is torn,
Your whispers float, like a gentle breeze,
Carrying promises, keys to unseen seas.

And as I lay, embraced by night's dark arms,
Surrendered to the sky's sparkling charms,
The whispers weave, through the fabric of space,
A bond unbroken, time cannot erase.

Glimpses of a Forgotten Realm

Beneath the veil of reality's guise,
Lies a realm where ancient mysteries rise,
Glimpses caught in the corner of an eye,
Of a forgotten world, beneath the earthly sky.

In dreams, it comes, vivid and clear,
A land where the past draws near,
Echoing footsteps of those long gone,
In the whispering winds, their silent song.

Through the mist of time, a vision unfolds,
Of towering citadels and streets of gold,
A fleeting glimpse of what once was,
Lost to time, without a cause.

Yet in the heart, the memory remains,
Of that distant realm, where magic reigns,
The glimpses grow stronger with each passing night,
A forgotten realm, brought briefly to light.

Serenade for the Starlit Wanderers

Under the canopy of night's embrace,
Where stars wander, in the void of space,
A serenade for those who roam,
In the endless sky, where dreams call home.

The moon, our guide, in the silent verse,
Bathes the world in a light, so diverse,
Singing a serenade, soft and clear,
For the starlit wanderers, drawing near.

With each note that in the darkness swirls,
The universe around us unfurls,
A symphony for the restless heart,
A promise that we're never apart.

So to you, who wander under starlit skies,
Carrying dreams in your eyes,
This serenade is for your flight,
A beacon in the deep, embracing night.

Architect of the Midnight Sky

In the realm of velvet skies,
Amid the silent, grand expanse,
Stars like scattered, glowing dyes,
Craft the night's intricate dance.

With every stroke of cosmic light,
Designs of unseen hands unfold,
In endless depths of the darkest night,
Silver and sapphire stories told.

Galaxies twirl in graceful arcs,
In the majestic night they lay,
Illuminating the eternal marks,
Of the architect's unseen sway.

Constellations in their ceaseless shift,
Trace the outlines of myth and lore,
In the sky, they gently drift,
A canvas vast, forevermore.

Each star a note in the symphony,
Played by the night, soft and high,
A testament to the mystery,
Of the architect of the midnight sky.

Carving Out the Night

With hands unseen, the night falls fast,
Upon the world in shadows cast,
The moon carves out its silvery path,
A silent guide, it shows its craft.

The stars assist in this grand scheme,
With twinkling eyes, they softly gleam,
Creating patterns, weaving dreams,
In the tapestry of night, they seem.

The cool, dark air whispers secrets untold,
Carrying tales of the bold,
The night, a sculptor of old,
Shapes the world in a mold.

Forests and fields lay quiet and still,
Under the night's gentle chill,
A vast canvas, at the moon's will,
Carved and shaped by skills so brill.

In every shadow and silvered light,
Lies the artistry of the night,
A symphony seen but by moon's sight,
In darkness, it finds its might.

Ballet of the Whispering Trees

Beneath the moon's gentle gaze,
The whispering trees begin their waltz,
Leaves rustle in the evening's haze,
In nature's ballroom, without faults.

Their branches sway in harmony,
To the soft music of the wind,
Invisible choreography,
By the night's hand, finely pinned.

Each leaf a dancer, light and free,
Twirling in the air with grace,
A performance only night can see,
In the secluded, sacred space.

The rustling grows, a crescendo soft,
A symphony of sight and sound,
The trees, their branches loft,
In this ballet, they are bound.

As dawn approaches, they slow their dance,
Whispers soft as a lover's glance,
The night recedes, day takes its chance,
But the ballet lives in the expanse.

Solitude in the Starlight

In the solitude of the starlight's glow,
I find myself, letting go,
Of the day's chaos, its endless flow,
Under the stars, I'm laid low.

The silver beams wash over me,
Cleansing thoughts, setting spirit free,
The night sky's vast, an endless sea,
In its depths, I lose the key.

Alone, but not in sorrow's hold,
With the stars, my fears unfold,
In the night, my heart grows bold,
As tales of ancient light are told.

The universe whispers in my ear,
Secrets of the cosmos, drawing near,
In this moment, nothing to fear,
For in the starlight, all is clear.

As dawn creeps, and night recedes,
In the starlight, I've sown my seeds,
Of dreams and hopes, of noble deeds,
In solitude, my soul feeds.

Shadows Bathing in Pale Light

Whispers float where shadows blend,
Casting tales that night does lend.
Underneath the pale moon's gaze,
Silence speaks in myriad ways.

Cloaked in dusk, the world transforms,
Ephemeral beauty performs.
Shadows dance on walls so tight,
Bathing all in ghostly light.

Serenade of cricket's song,
Fills the air where dreams belong.
Moonbeams touch the earth's soft bed,
Kissing shadows that we tread.

Through the night, their dance does weave,
In the light, we scarcely believe.
Yet in these hours, dark and slight,
Find peace in pale, silvery light.

Waltz of the Enchanted Glade

In the glade where whispers call,
Nature holds her nightly ball.
Moonlit streams of silver thread,
Guide the dance where footsteps tread.

Elves and sprites in circles bound,
To the flute's enchanting sound.
Trees sway gently, in delight,
Under stars, the glade alight.

Ferns and flowers form the floor,
Magic breathes from every pore.
Creatures of the night convene,
In this scene, as if a dream.

With each step, the earth gives thanks,
Rivers curtsy, breeze plays pranks.
Ever in this enchanted dance,
In the glade, we find our chance.

Veiled in Midnight's Mystery

Veiled in shadows, night does keep,
Secrets that in sunlight sleep.
Midnight's cloak, so dark and deep,
Holds the dreams that we seek to reap.

Stars peek out from velvet skies,
Watching over with gentle eyes.
Through the darkness, whispers rise,
Telling tales of old, wise lies.

Moonlight filters through the trees,
Casting spells with silent ease.
In the cool and gentle breeze,
Mysteries flow like the seas.

Beneath the veil, we dare to tread,
Drawn to what the night has spread.
The unknown paths we come to prise,
Underneath the starlit skies.

Eyes Glimmering with Stardust

In the depth of night so pure,
Eyes glimmer with a light so sure.
Reflecting stars, they hold a lure,
Tales of dreams that long endure.

Like cosmos vast, in gaze profound,
Each soul's a universe unbound.
In eyes, the universe is found,
With stardust, their dreams are crowned.

Gaze into the night's embrace,
And find therein a sacred space.
Where hopes and dreams we dare to chase,
In stardust eyes, the stars we trace.

So let your gaze, to heavens cast,
Ponder mysteries, vast and vast.
For in those eyes, the night is past,
And dreams with stardust, everlast.

Watching Over the Still Waters

Above the silent, glassy lake,
Where shadows dance and light does break,
A whispering breeze begins to wake,
Guarding dreams that we partake.

Beneath the moon's watchful eye,
Stars reflect, in water lie,
Secrets told in silence, by,
The night's own tender, sighing cry.

Ripples form with gentle ease,
Carrying thoughts like autumn leaves,
Over waters calm and deep,
Promises the heavens keep.

In this moment, time stands still,
Nature's beauty, a tranquil thrill,
Watching over, with a will,
Peace lies here, serene and chill.

Secrets Within the Silver Gleam

In moonlight's silver, secrets gleam,
Whispering tales of a forgotten dream,
Where shadows play and nothing's as it seem,
In this dance, does the unseen teem.

Each beam a thread in night's quilt sewn,
Casting spells where light is shown,
A canvas painted, a mystery grown,
In silver whispers, the night has flown.

Beneath the glow, secrets find their way,
Through the cracks of the mundane, they stray,
A silver gleam to lead the day,
Back to where magic lays.

In the gleam, hopes are spun,
Under the watchful eye of the moon and sun,
Till the night's magic, day has won,
In silver's secret, we are one.

Parables Spun by the Dark

In the velvet cloak of night,
Where stars tell tales by their light,
Darkness spins with sheer delight,
Parables of might and plight.

Ancient stories hidden deep,
In the night, they do not sleep,
Whispers that through the darkness creep,
Secrets that the shadows keep.

Tales of old, a warning, a sign,
Beneath the moon's pale, ghostly shine,
Where truth and lore intertwine,
In the dark, their edges are fine.

By the night's enigmatic art,
Stories flow from heart to heart,
In each ending, a new start,
Parables spun and then depart.

Enveloped by the Night's Whisper

When night descends, softly, a shroud,
And moonlight breaks through the cloud,
Whispers float, in darkness, proud,
As the night its peace endowed.

In silence, the world seems to speak,
With words that through the twilight leak,
Each whisper, a promise to seek,
Strength and solace for the weak.

The night's whisper, a gentle balm,
Underneath its tranquil calm,
A world apart, a healing psalm,
In the quietude, a soothing qualm.

Nature listens, so profound,
In every tree, rock, and mound,
With every whisper, we are bound,
By night's embrace, we are found.

Temples of the Sky

Above the earth, in realms so high,
Where eagles soar and spirits fly.
Majestic peaks in sunlight lie,
Nature's spires, aiming for the sky.

Ether's home on mountains' sigh,
Whispers of the ancients, by and by.
In every dawn, the sun's new try,
Temples of the sky, where dreams don't die.

Clouds embrace these peaks so shy,
Casting shadows, time draws nigh.
These silent sentinels, in the eye
Of storms, stand strong, they do not lie.

Rooted deep, their secrets ply,
In sacred stones, under the sky.
History's voices, in winds that cry,
Echoing through the temples of the sky.

In night's embrace, the stars draw high,
Guiding souls gently, they signify.
The endless cycle, in the sky,
Nature's temples, where peace does lie.

The Indigo Blanket

Under the indigo blanket, wide and deep,
The world in silence, seems to sleep.
Moonbeams dance, their vigil keep,
Over the secrets that the shadows peep.

Stars stitch patterns, in the night they weave,
Across the fabric, dreams they conceive.
A tapestry of cosmos, that few believe,
Under the indigo blanket, we receive.

Mysteries unfold in the dark's embrace,
Whispers of the universe, in endless space.
Each a glowing ember, in its rightful place,
Under the indigo blanket, with grace.

The night's quilt covers, gentle, bleak,
Holding stories that the heavens speak.
In its folds, the curious seek,
The wonders of the night, unique.

Silent wishes on shooting stars leap,
Into the heart of the night, they seep.
Under the indigo blanket, secrets keep,
In the quiet, the world does weep.

The Never-Ending Dusk

In the twilight of the never-ending dusk,
Colors blend, in the world's husk.
The sun dips low, in trust,
Leaving behind the day, now just a musk.

Shadows stretch, reaching long,
The moment lingers, a silent song.
Time stands still, nothing wrong,
In the never-ending dusk, where dreams belong.

Horizon's line, blurred and meek,
Hiding tales that the twilight seek.
Every sunset, unique,
A story of the never-ending dusk, to speak.

In this realm, where light gently treads,
Between the day and night, it spreads.
A canvas painted in fleeting reds,
Where the heart of mystery, its thread weds.

The dusk, a bridge, a gentle sigh,
Between the earth and the sprawling sky.
In its beauty, our Spirits fly,
Under the gaze of the never-ending dusk's eye.

Enigma of the Celestial Spheres

In the vastness of the night's embrace,
The stars, a map, in darkness trace.
Ancient lights in the endless space,
The enigma of the celestial spheres, in grace.

Orbiting in silence, a dance so fine,
Planets align, in a design divine.
Galaxies swirl, in mysteries' line,
Woven by time, a cosmic sign.

Asters and comets, in their flight,
Crossing the void, a trail so bright.
Every moment, a breathtaking sight,
Unveiling secrets of the night.

The moon watches, serene and aloof,
Guardian of tides, from her roof.
In her cycles, the oceans' proof,
The celestial spheres, enigmatic and aloof.

In this universe, vast and unknown,
We stand beneath the stars, alone.
Yet connected, in the vast unknown,
By the enigma of the spheres, shown.

Dance of the Silvery Glow

In the moon's tender light, so fair,
Where whispers trace the cool night air,
Each step a twirl, a fluid grace,
In silvery glow, they embrace.

Beneath the vast, celestial dome,
In night's embrace, where dreamers roam,
The dance unfolds, free and aglow,
With every move, their spirits grow.

With pirouettes on dew-kissed ground,
The night alive with muted sound,
The dancers merge with lunar rays,
In harmony, their bodies sway.

The world, a stage of endless night,
Bears witness to this pure delight,
As all around, the stars conspire,
To kindle dreams with silvery fire.

Maiden of the Starlight

In twilight's embrace, she softly treads,
Where starlight weaves through cosmic threads,
Her eyes agleam with distant dreams,
Her presence sewn with starlit seams.

She dances where the shadows play,
In realms where night outshines the day,
Her gown, a weave of moonbeam's lace,
Adorned with the night's gentle grace.

Through galaxies in her gaze concealed,
A universe, in her eyes revealed,
Each step, a passage through the skies,
Where silent whispers of cosmos lies.

With every turn, a star is born,
From twilight till the break of dawn,
The maiden's dance, a sacred rite,
The cosmos veiled in her starlight.

Shadows Cast by Hidden Light

In the quiet where shadows fall,
Beside the light that cloaks them all,
There whispers a tale of hidden might,
Of shadows cast by hidden light.

Beneath the gleam that all can see,
The darkness holds a mystery,
Where every fear and dream takes flight,
A dance of dark, a dance of light.

These silhouettes, both bold and shy,
Stretch forth their hands to touch the sky,
A canvas vast for night's pure sight,
Where stars gaze back with hidden light.

So in the dim, let hearts not fright,
For in the dark, there's wisdom's bite,
From shadows cast, our souls ignite,
To find our paths by hidden light.

The Pulse of the Ancient

In the heart of the ageless land,
Where history's layers expand,
The pulse of the ancient still beats,
In whispers on winds, it repeats.

The stones, the trees, the endless sands,
Hold tales from far and mystic lands,
The drumming earth beneath our feet,
Recites the past in rhythms sweet.

Each echo of the ancient's call,
Through time's thick veil, to us, does fall,
A legacy, both vast and deep,
In this embrace, our spirits leap.

For we are but a moment's light,
In the ancient's endless night,
Yet in their pulse, we find our own,
A connection to the unknown.

Entwined with the Night's Mystery

Under the cloak of night's deep hue,
We tread softly, the world anew.
Stars our guides, whispers our light,
In dreamscape's fold, we take our flight.

Secrets veiled in the dark's embrace,
With every shadow, we trace.
The moon's glow, our silent ally,
In its mystery, we willingly comply.

Echoes of the night, subtly entwined,
In its enigma, our spirits find.
A solace in the velvet sky,
Where our silent wishes lie.

Boundless, in the night's deep thrall,
We answer to its ancient call.
With every breath, we're drawn in deep,
In the night's mystery, secrets we keep.

Midnight's Silver Caress

In the silent hours of night's peak,
The stars whisper, the heavens speak.
A silver light bathes the land,
Midnight's touch, a gentle hand.

The world sleeps under night's soft gaze,
In dreams, lost in a timeless maze.
But with the moon's gentle caress,
We find beauty in the night's stillness.

A river of silver flows in the dark,
Guiding the lost, igniting a spark.
Midnight's embrace, tender and sweet,
In its quietude, our hearts meet.

Under this spellbinding silver light,
All seems hopeful, all feels right.
The world, under a tranquil spell,
In midnight's caress, we wish to dwell.

Whispers in Lunar Shadows

When the moon casts shadows long,
In the stillness, we hear their song.
Whispers carried on the night's cool breath,
Tales of love, life, and death.

Each shadow tells a different tale,
Of dreams that soared, of dreams that failed.
But in the lunar light, all find grace,
In the silver gleam, a sacred space.

Through the leaves, the moonlight dances,
In its glow, every shadow enchances.
Whispers in the night, a chorus so profound,
In their stories, our own are found.

Lunar shadows stretch across the land,
A gentle touch, a soft command.
In their embrace, we find release,
In the whispers of the night, we find our peace.

Crescent's Quiet Beckoning

A crescent moon in the starlit sky,
A silent call, a soft sigh.
In its light, a path revealed,
To the heart's quiet field.

In this glow, dreams whisper clear,
Guided by the night, we have no fear.
The crescent's curve, a gentle embrace,
In its serenity, we find our place.

Through the night, this quiet guide,
Leads us where true selves reside.
Under its watch, we may roam free,
In its light, we truly see.

The crescent beckons, a call to explore,
Beyond the day's loud roar.
In its subtle light, we tread lightly,
Bound for realms where dreams shine brightly.

Embracing the Nocturne

Under the cloak of the night's embrace,
Where dreams and reality interlace,
Stars whisper secrets, old and profound,
In their light, mysteries abound.

The moon, a sentinel in the vast skies,
Guides the lost with benevolent eyes,
Its silver beams, a path so clear,
In the nocturne, we find no fear.

Owls sing hymns in the cool night air,
Their melodies slice the thick despair,
A serenade for the souls awake,
In darkness, solace we partake.

The world sleeps under night's soft shroud,
But in our hearts, adventures avowed,
Embracing the nocturne, we silently roam,
In the kingdom of stars, we find our home.

Mirror of the Cosmos

In the night sky, a mirror so vast,
Reflecting cosmos from ages past,
Each star, a story engraved in light,
A celestial dance, a marvelous sight.

Galaxies swirl in an endless waltz,
Bound by gravity, time, and faults,
The universe whispers in hues so bright,
Unlocking secrets in the veil of night.

Planets align in harmonious grace,
A symphony of spheres in the vast space,
In this cosmic mirror, we see our fate,
On the canvas of time, we inscribe our date.

A reflection of us in the stars above,
A tapestry of life, woven with love,
In the cosmic mirror, we find our place,
A small part of the universe's embrace.

Pathway to the Unknown

Beyond the edges of our known map,
Lies a pathway, an unseen gap,
An invitation to the brave and bold,
To uncover mysteries untold.

Down this path, shadows play,
Where light and dark have their fray,
Whispers of the past guide our way,
To the threshold of night and day.

The unknown calls with a siren's song,
Drawing us where the brave belong,
In the heart of the unexplored,
Lies the treasure, the untold reward.

With each step, history unfurls,
New worlds revealed, as the pathway swirls,
In the unknown, we find our quest,
To seek, to discover, to never rest.

Threads of Silver Light

In the tapestry of the night's sky,
Threads of silver light softly lie,
Weaving patterns of dreams and fate,
In their glow, our hearts resonate.

Moonbeams dance on leaves and lakes,
A silent ballet that the night awakes,
In this moment, time seems to bend,
Under silver threads, our spirits ascend.

Stars entwine in celestial array,
Guiding travelers on their way,
In silver threads, hope is spun,
Under the watchful gaze of the sun.

Through the fabric of night and day,
Silver threads show us the way,
A lustrous guide, gentle and light,
In their embrace, our dreams take flight.

A Silent Ode to Twilight's Pearl

As dusk enfolds the quiet earth,
A silent ode begins its birth.
Twilight's pearl in somber gleam,
Whispers secrets to the stream.

Upon the hills where shadows play,
The last light kisses day away.
Stars awaken in the hush,
Underneath the evening's blush.

Gentle breezes carry dreams,
Through the night, a soft moonbeam.
Reflects on waters, still and deep,
Guiding the world into sleep.

In silence, beauty finds its voice,
In twilight's pearl, hearts rejoice.
A moment caught in time's embrace,
A tranquil, sweet, ethereal place.

Harvest of the Night Sky

In the velvet cloak of nightfall's embrace,
Stars scatter across the celestial space.
A farmer of dreams begins to sow,
In the harvest of the night sky, they glow.

Each star, a seed of distant light,
Sprouts across the canvas of night.
A tapestry woven with silver thread,
Upon which our deepest hopes are spread.

The moon, a shepherd, gentle and fair,
Guides these dreams with tender care.
Herds the stars, the constellations bright,
In the pasture of the dark, she brings light.

Harvest of wishes, dreams taking flight,
Beneath the dome of the shadowed night.
With every star that falls, a tale is told,
In the night sky's harvest, our dreams unfold.

Tides Swayed by Invisible Hands

In the realm where silent waters flow,
Tides are swayed by hands unseen.
Mysteries that the moon does know,
In the dance of night and day, so keen.

Push and pull, a silent symphony,
Crafted by the moon's soft glow.
A ballet beneath the sea's canopy,
Guided by the currents ebb and flow.

Waves whisper secrets to the shore,
Invisible hands sculpting sand.
The moon, a maestro, conducting more,
In its command, the sea expands.

Each tide, a verse in nature's song,
Swayed by forces strong and grand.
In this dance, we all belong,
Held in the invisible hand's command.

Phases of the Heart's Longing

Like the moon, our hearts did wax and wane,
In phases of longing, joy, and pain.
New beginnings, a crescent in the dark,
A sliver of hope, a newfound spark.

Full of love, when our hearts are bright,
Shining with all their might.
Yet wanes again, to the void we face,
In the cycle, we find our place.

Eclipsed by shadows, love may hide,
But in the dark, new dreams abide.
A cycle unbroken, through time's vast sea,
The heart's longing, eternally free.

Through each phase, our love's tale spun,
From dawn's first light to the setting sun.
In the heart's longing, we find our truth,
In every age, from old to youth.

Chorus of the Ethereal

In whispers soft, the heavens sigh,
A gentle song, the stars comply.
A chorus vast, of night's embrace,
Each note a touch of ethereal grace.

Through veils unseen, the melodies flow,
A dance of light, in the dark they glow.
A symphony of dreams aloft,
In celestial whispers, tender and soft.

The moon, a maestro in the sky,
Guides the stars as they soar and fly.
An ethereal chorus, pure and clear,
In the silence of night, it draws near.

In the quiet heart of the sleeping earth,
A gentle hymn of celestial birth.
A song of peace, of tranquil rest,
In the chorus of the ethereal, we're blessed.

The Night's Mesmeric Spell

Under the cloak of the evening's allure,
The night casts its spell, mysterious and pure.
Stars twinkle softly, in rhythms they tell,
Stories of ages, in the night's mesmeric spell.

The moon whispers secrets to a darkened sea,
Waves hum in response, in tranquil harmony.
A spellbinding dance, where shadows dwell,
Embraced by the enchantment of the night's swell.

Creatures of darkness, in the moonlight bask,
In the splendor of twilight, they wear their mask.
The night's gentle breath, a soothing well,
In its quietude, our restless thoughts quell.

In the embrace of dusk, worries unfurl,
As the night spins its tales, a mystical swirl.
A canvas of dreams, where fantasies gel,
Under the mesmerizing spell, all is well.

Reflections Beyond the Dark

In the depths of the night, where shadows play,
A glimmer of hope flickers far away.
Beyond the dark, a silent plea,
Reflections of what is yet to be.

Amidst the echo of forgotten cries,
A spark of clarity in the night skies.
Illuminating paths that lead astray,
Guiding lost souls to find their way.

In the heart of darkness, a radiant sight,
A beacon of love, in the blackest night.
Reflections beyond the dark, a shimmering lake,
Mirror of the soul, where dreams awake.

With each reflection, a lesson learned,
In the depths of darkness, bridges burned.
A journey through the night, into the light,
Where reflections beyond the dark shine bright.

The Gown of Twilight

As daylight fades and dusk takes its bow,
The sky adorns its gown of twilight now.
A tapestry of purple, orange, and pink,
In the evening light, the world stops to think.

The horizon dresses in its finest hue,
A moment of peace, as the night breaks through.
Stars peek through the fabric, a gleam so slight,
Adorning the gown with diamonds bright.

The whisper of nightfall, a tranquil lull,
As darkness enfolds the world in its pull.
The gown of twilight, a sight so divine,
Marks the end of the day, with a sign so fine.

In the quiet of dusk, as shadows merge,
The gown of twilight begins to surge.
A transformation from day to night,
In the gown of twilight, the world finds its light.

Reflections in the Still Water

In the mirror of the lake, under the sky's sheen,
Where the world upside down, appears serene,
Each wave tells a story, a whisper, a sigh,
In the silence, our truths and secrets lie.

Reflected in the still water, so clear,
The beauty of the heavens, suddenly near,
Mountains bow their heads to see their grace,
In this tranquil, undisturbed resting place.

The trees lean over, yearning for a glance,
At their own trembling leaves, as if in a trance,
Birds skim the surface, touching their twin,
Unity in reflection, outside and within.

As the sun dips low, setting the sky afire,
Colors blend and dance, reaching higher,
The water holds the inferno in its embrace,
A fleeting beauty, in the still water's space.

When night descends, and stars take their place,
The lake becomes a portal to outer space,
Reflecting a universe, vast and divine,
In its depths, the cosmos and earth entwine.

Orbiting the Edges of Madness

In the orbit of thoughts, where madness lies,
We dance on the edge, where sanity flies,
Round and round, in a ceaseless spin,
Touching the void, where ends begin.

Whispers in the dark, too faint to hear,
Grow louder at the edge, feeding the fear,
Each whisper a spark, igniting the mind,
In the dance of the mad, what truths we find.

Eyes wide open, in the night's embrace,
Seeing beyond, what we face to face,
The edge of madness, a delicate line,
Where dreams and nightmares intertwine.

Grasping at shadows, reaching for light,
Orbiting the edges, in perpetual flight,
The mind a universe, vast and unknown,
At the brink of madness, we're not alone.

In the silent echo, of the unspoken,
Madness and sanity, forever woven,
On the edge we stand, looking in,
Embracing the chaos, within the din.

The Painter of Nocturnal Blooms

With a palette of shadows, and moonlight in hand,
The painter stirs the night, across the land,
Nocturnal blooms, in hues so deep,
Whisper secrets, that the daylight will keep.

Under the cloak of night, with stars as guides,
He paints in silence, where mystery resides,
The canvas, alive, with each stroke and sway,
Blooms that fade at the first light of day.

Glistening dew, on petals portrayed,
In colors of the night, not to fade,
Each flower, a story, a nocturnal dream,
Captured in the silence, by the moonbeam.

Through the dark forest, and the meadows wide,
The painter wanders, with the night by his side,
Leaving behind, in the wake of his roam,
Blooms of the night, in their shadowy home.

As dawn approaches, and paints the sky anew,
The nocturnal blooms, bid the night adieu,
But the painter smiles, at the coming of the light,
For he knows he'll paint again, with the next night's sight.

Tales Woven in the Celestial Tapestry

In the weave of the night sky, stories untold,
Where stars and planets, in beauty, unfold,
Each a thread, in the tapestry vast,
Holding tales of the present, future, and past.

Constellations dance, in patterns divine,
Narrating myths, of origins and time,
The tales of gods, heroes bold and fair,
Weaved into the night, with celestial care.

Across the expanse, nebulae swirl and twine,
In colors that stories and mysteries define,
Galaxies spinning, in an endless waltz,
Each turn a tale, in the cosmic vaults.

Meteor showers, the weavers' swift needles,
Stitching the sky, with stories of peoples,
A canvas so vast, where the universe writes,
Its history, its future, in the dark of the nights.

So look up above, when the night falls serene,
And read the tales, in the celestial scene,
For every star, a story does keep,
In the boundless library, of the night sky deep.

Milton Keynes UK
Ingram Content Group UK Ltd.
UKHW021806020624
443470UK00005BA/33